Hitler & National Socialism

Martyn Whittock

Heinemann Library,
Halley Court, Jordan Hill, Oxford OX2 8EJ
a division of Reed Educational and Professional
Publishing Ltd

OXFORD LONDON EDINBURGH MADRID
ATHENS BOLOGNA PARIS MELBOURNE
SYDNEY AUCKLAND SINGAPORE TOKYO
IBADAN NAIROBI HARARE GABORONE
PORTSMOUTH NH (USA)

First published 1995

96 97 98 10 9 8 7 6 5 4 3 2

**British Library Cataloguing Data is available
from the British Library on request.**

ISBN 0 431 07072 5

Designed by Ron Kamen, Green Door Design Ltd,
Basingstoke

Illustrated by Jeff Edwards and Douglas Hall

Printed in Spain by Mateu Cromo

The front cover shows a Nazi Rally during the 1930s.

Acknowledgements

The author and publisher would like to thank the
following for permission to reproduce photographs:

AKG London: 1.6
ET Archive: 5.6
Stacy RosenstockFormat: 7.3
Gemeente Leeuwarden: 6.4
Gunn Brinson: 3.1
Hulton Deutsch: 2.5, 4.3
Imperial War Museum: 1.5, 2.8, 3.14
Popperfoto: 3.11, 4.8, 5.11
Topham Picture Source: Cover
Weimar Archive: 3.6, 3.10

Every effort has been made to contact copyright
holders of material published in this book. Any
omissions will be rectified in subsequent printings if
notice is given to the publisher.

*To my good friend, Christopher Macer, who also hopes
for a more just and kinder world.*

Note

In this book some of the words are printed in bold
type. This indicates that the word is listed in the
glossary on pages 46–7. The glossary gives a brief
explanation of words that may be new to you.

Details of written sources

In some sources the wording or sentence structure
has been simplified to ensure that the source is
accessible.

Alan Bullock, *Hitler and Stalin: Parallel Lives*,
HarperCollins, 1991: 1.1, 1.3, 2.4, 6.2, 6.3, 6.5, 6.7, 6.8
Brian Catchpole, *A Map History of the Modern World*,
Heinemann, 1982: 5.15
Christopher Culpin, *Making History: World History
from 1914 to the Present Day*, Collins, 1984: 5.1
M. N. Duffy, *The Twentieth Century*, Basil Blackwell,
1983: 5.2
B. Engelmann, *In Hitler's Germany*, Mandarin, 1989:
2.9, 3.2, 3.3, 3.15, 3.16, 4.5, 4.6, 4.7, 4.10, 5.5, 5.7, 5.9
J. Fest, *The Face of the Third Reich*, Pelican, 1972: 3.4
C. Fitzgibbon (trans), *Commandant of Auschwitz*,
Weidenfeld and Nicolson, 1953: 6.9
R. Gibson and J. Nichol, *Germany*, Blackwell, 1985:
2.7
A. Hitler, *Mein Kampf* (translated by R. Manheim),
Pimlico, 1992: 1.8, 5.8
H. Hohne, *Order of the Death's Head*, Pan, 1972: 6.6
I. Kershaw, *Profiles in Power*, Longman, 1991: 1.7, 2.3
I. Kershaw, *The Nazi Dictatorship*, Longman 1989:
4.14
J. Laver, *Imperial and Weimar Germany*, Hodder and
Stoughton, 1992: 2.1, 2.2
S. Lee, *Nazi Germany*, Heinemann, 1989: 3.7
R. Manvell, *The Conspirators*, Pan / Ballantyne, 1971:
5.14
H. Mills, *Twentieth Century World History in Focus*,
Macmillan, 1984: 4.11, 5.4
J. Noakes and G. Pridham, *Nazism 1919–1945*,
Exeter University Press, 1984: 3.5
K. Perry, *Britain and the European Community*,
Heinemann, 1984: 7.2
Joe Scott, *The World Since 1914*, Heinemann, 1989:
4.15, 5.16
Jane Shuter (Ed), *Christabel Bielenberg and Nazi
Germany*, Heinemann, 1994: 2.6, 3.12, 5.10
Paul Shuter and Terry Lewis, *Skills in History 3*,
Heinemann, 1988: 4.12
W. Simpson, *Hitler and Germany*, Cambridge
University Press, 1991: 1.2
L. Snellgrove, *The Modern World Since 1870*,
Longman, 1979: 1.4, 7.1
A. J. P. Taylor, *Origins of the Second World War*,
Penguin, 1961: 4.16
G. Weinberg, *The Foreign Policy of Hitler's Germany*,
1980: 4.13

Contents

UNIT 1

Who was Adolf Hitler?

This book is about the life of Adolf Hitler, who was the leader of the **Nazi Party** and the ruler of Germany from 1933 to 1945. Together with the people who agreed with his ideas he was responsible for destroying the lives of millions of people and changing the course of 20th century history.

To try to understand a person like Hitler, we need to ask questions about his background. What was happening in Europe at the time of his birth? What was his early family life like? What sort of things happened to him which may have influenced his beliefs and future actions?

Important events in Europe in the late nineteenth century

There were millions of German-speaking people living in Europe, but they did not all live in the same country. Some lived in Austria which was part of the Austro-Hungarian Empire; others lived outside of this Empire in states such as Prussia, Bavaria and Saxony. During the 19th century there was great rivalry between Prussia and Austria; both wanted to be the most powerful German-speaking country in Europe.

The Unification of Germany

In 1862, Otto von Bismarck became the chief minister of Prussia. Under his direction Prussia fought a number of successful wars between 1864 and 1871 and brought the smaller German states into a unified German Empire. Austria was deliberately kept out of the new German Empire by Bismarck. He wanted to make sure that the power of Prussia was not challenged.

The German Empire was ruled from Berlin, the capital city of Prussia. The head of state was the **Kaiser** (Emperor). Although there was a parliament (the **Reichstag**) the Kaiser had more say in running the country. He was not at all keen on **democracy** where ordinary people elected the government. The new Germany was very powerful and a force to be reckoned with. It had a strong army and was one of the world's main industrial powers – second only to the USA. Many of its people were fierce **nationalists**. They were very **patriotic** and believed Germany was superior to any other country.

The Austro-Hungarian Empire

The huge Austro-Hungarian Empire was situated in central Europe. The Empire contained many different racial groups including Germans, Czechs, Poles, and Slovaks; there were also numerous Jewish people of different nationalities. Most German people in the Empire lived in Austria. For centuries the Germans had enjoyed a position of superiority over the other groups. German was the official language and all of the top positions in the government were filled by Germans. The Czechs, Slovaks and Poles had very little say in the running of the government.

Not surprisingly, these peoples started to demand equality. The Czechs, in particular, said they should be allowed to run their own affairs. The Austrian government showed signs of giving in to these demands and this angered many Germans. The Germans feared they were going to lose their influence and became hostile to the other racial groups.

The birth of Hitler

Hitler was born in 1889 in the small Austrian town of Braunau-am-Inn, situated on the border between Austria and Bavaria (see map). Hitler was German-speaking and a subject of the Austro-Hungarian Empire. However, he was born at a time when the Empire was in trouble. Many Germans were very afraid that they were losing their privileged position within the Empire. There was racial tension and distrust. Street-fighting between the different groups was on the increase.

In 1893 the Pan German League was formed. It called for Germans to break away from the Austro-Hungarian Empire and join with the new German Empire. The League said that all the German people in Europe should be part of the same country. These arguments increased the tension in Austria. This was the atmosphere of prejudice and jealousy in which the young Hitler grew up.

SOURCE 1

Hitler became a rabid German nationalist but, instead of sharing in the confidence of the new German Empire ruled from Berlin, he took on the anxious outlook of the Germans within the Austro-Hungarian Empire.

Alan Bullock, Hitler and Stalin: Parallel Lives, 1991.

SOURCE 2

Hitler drew on German traditions for three of his ideas:
- his belief in the superiority of the German race
- his dislike of democracy
- his anti-Semitism [anti-Jewish beliefs], which had roots deep in European as well as German history.

W. Simpson, Hitler and Germany, 1991.

Where most German-speaking people lived in Europe, 1900.

Hitler – his early years of frustration and disappointment

Hitler was the child of an elderly father (Alois) and a much younger mother (Klara). His father was a customs officer and, although Hitler later claimed to have come from a poor background, the family was quite well-off. Alois and Klara did not have a happy marriage. Alois was a hard father who took little interest in his children. He was often bad tempered. Adolf was much closer to his mother who seems to have spoiled him. In 1938 Hitler had the village where his father was buried turned into an army training ground. Clearly he had few loving memories of Alois. Hitler, however, did inherit his father's uncaring attitude towards people he thought were 'weak'.

The Hitler family moved house several times and Adolf went to a number of different schools. At the age of 11 he went to the secondary school at Linz. He did badly in most subjects. Only in drawing did he gain satisfactory marks. Historians of Hitler's early life claim he was lazy and rude. Hitler, however, had an inflated opinion of himself. He thought he was an artistic genius and he was frustrated that he did not get greater credit from his teachers. Hitler left school in 1905 without being awarded his leavers' certificate. He was not interested in getting a job; instead he lived off his mother, dreaming of becoming a great artist. His only friend was August Kubizek. Hitler spent hours reading books about German history. They said that the German race was superior to others and the Jews, in particular, were inferior. There was no basis at all for such ideas but Hitler came to believe them.

In 1907 Hitler and Kubizek went to live in Vienna, the capital city of Austria. Hitler wanted to train to be an artist. He tried for a place at the Vienna Academy of Fine Arts but failed to pass the entry examination. In contrast, Kubizek gained entry to the Vienna Music Academy. In 1908 Hitler made a second application for the Art Academy. Again, he was unsuccessful. Such was his anger he could not face his friend. He moved out of the flat he shared with Kubizek and became a tramp.

Hitler's failure led to six unhappy years of loneliness and anger. He had no direction in his life, no close friends and relied on charities for food. From 1910 onwards, he lived in dosshouses and earned money by selling postcards he had copied. Fellow-tramps thought of him as a man with fanatical opinions who could only shout at those he disagreed with. Hitler refused to look for a proper job, blaming others for his bad luck.

SOURCE 3

The importance of Hitler's time in Vienna lies in two things. The first is that Hitler did not abandon his self esteem. The fact that he preserved it over six long years shows the strength of will which was to prove the foundation of his political success. At the same time he continued to experience frustration and humiliation, which fed his desire for revenge on the world which rejected him. As a result of his experiences in Vienna his ideas about the world began to take shape.

A. Bullock, Hitler and Stalin: Parallel Lives, 1991.

SOURCE 4

Because of his miserable experiences, Hitler grew to hate Vienna. Its mixture of races – Jews, Slovaks and Czechs – irritated him. Like most Austrians he despised these people and loved everything German. In particular he became infected with the Viennese dislike of Jews, and this terrible prejudice remained with him all his life.

L. Snellgrove, The Modern World Since 1870, 1979.

Hitler in the Odeonsplatz, Munich 1914, cheering the start of war.

Most of all he blamed the Jews. At the time there were almost 200,000 Jews living in Vienna. Hitler became jealous of the richer Jews who lived in large mansions and frightened of the poorer ones, many of whom were immigrants from Poland. He read anti-Semitic (anti-Jewish) leaflets and pamphlets which strengthened his prejudice.

Other groups also angered Hitler. He had no time for **communism** and **socialism** which said that everyone should be equal. To Hitler this was not the case. He firmly believed that there was a 'pecking-order' of races with the Germans at the top. In addition, the communists said that all working people, regardless of their country, should join together against the bosses and factory owners. Again Hitler disagreed. He believed that belonging to the German nation was much more important than belonging to a 'class'.

In 1913 he moved to Munich in Germany, and was there when war broke out in 1914. War offered him excitement and the chance to break away from his miserable day-to-day existence.

LUEGER

Karl Lueger (1844–1910) was elected onto Vienna's municipal council in 1875 and became famous for fighting corruption. He won the support of the better-off working class (who feared the other nationalities in the Austro-Hungarian Empire) with speeches attacking Jews and supporting the rights of Germans throughout the Empire. This had a great influence on Hitler. He ignored the fact that Lueger also wanted all nationalities in the Empire to share power and be treated equally.

From 1897, Lueger was mayor of Vienna. He had gas and electricity supplied and set up parks, schools and hospitals.

Hitler and colleagues recovering from their wounds in 1916.

The effects of the First World War on Hitler

Immediately war broke out in 1914, Hitler volunteered to fight for the German army and was overjoyed when he was accepted (he had earlier been rejected as unfit for service in the Austrian army). He arrived on the Western Front in October 1914 and took part in heavy fighting at the first Battle of Ypres. He remained at the front for two years as a 'front-line' fighter until he was wounded in 1916.

Hitler enjoyed life in the German army. He now felt he had a purpose in life. He was dedicated to destroying the enemies of the German people. This suited his passionate belief that German- speaking people were superior to all others. To fight for Germany made him feel important and no longer a failure.

The comradeship of soldiers in the trenches suited his personality. They were linked in a common cause without the need to have close personal relationships. Many of the German front-line fighters went on to join the Nazi Party in the 1920s.

Hitler was a messenger-carrier for his regiment. He was regarded as brave and won the Iron Cross, First Class, a rare honour for an ordinary soldier. He rose to the rank of corporal, but his officers did not think he was suitable for further promotion.

But Hitler annoyed his comrades by his support for the war and his obvious enjoyment of it. He rarely took home leave and showed no interest in anything apart from the war. In October 1918, as Germany was on the brink of losing the war, he was caught in a gas attack and temporarily blinded.

The end of the war and Hitler's reaction

Hitler was in hospital when he heard the news of the German surrender in November 1918. He was horrified. In 1917 he had been appalled by those Germans who wanted to end the war. Now it seemed to him that these 'traitors' had succeeded. Hitler refused to believe that the army had been beaten. Instead, he found it easier to believe that Germany had been betrayed by Jews and communists who had not been fighting at the front. He believed that Germany was in terrible danger of being destroyed and this thought angered him greatly. On leaving hospital Hitler returned to Munich.

SOURCE 8

I staggered back to my ward and dug my burning head into my blanket and pillow. Since the day when I had stood at my mother's grave I had not wept. But now I could not help it. All personal suffering vanishes in comparison with the misfortunes of Germany. So the war had been in vain. All the sacrifices, the hunger and thirst, the shame of indignation and disgrace burned my brow. Hatred grew in me, hatred for those responsible for this deed. Kaiser Wilhelm II held out the hand of friendship to the communists without thinking that the scoundrels have no honour. While they still held the Kaiser's hand in theirs, their own hand was reaching for the dagger. There is no making pacts with Jews.

A. Hitler, Mein Kampf, 1925. Hitler is describing his reaction to news of Germany's defeat.

SOURCE 7

The war was a crucial formative period for Hitler, an experience which strengthened his already existing prejudices and burning obsessions. News of the German defeat was a stunning blow. He was temporarily traumatised and unhinged. The hatred which had been welling within now burst ferociously into the open.

I. Kershaw, Profiles in Power: Hitler, 1991.

KAISER WILHEIM II

Kaiser Wilhelm II (1859–1941) became ruler of Germany and Prussia in 1888. He had no clear idea how to run Germany, and made this worse by dismissing Bismarck, who had advised Wilheim's father so well. Wilheim promised reforms to the working class people of Germany, but did very little. This made him unpopular, as did breaking off Germany's alliance with Russia. This led to an alliance between Russia and Germany's enemy, France.

He decided that he would have to make Germany a stronger world power. He and Admiral Tirpitz strengthened the navy, to compete with Britain. He tried to build up an overseas empire. When war broke out in 1914 he joined in on the side of Austria. He was not involved in the planning of the war, and was blamed for Germany being on the losing side and the disastrous terms for peace which followed. He was forced to abdicate on 9 November, 1918.

Why did the Nazis succeed?

The Weimar Republic

On 9 November 1918 the Kaiser fled to Holland and Germany was proclaimed a **republic**. The Reichstag was left with the job of running Germany. This new German government began its rule at Weimar in February 1919, which is why it was called the Weimar Republic. The government agreed to end the war. This was very unpopular because many Germans were not aware that the war had been going badly. They believed that the army could have fought on but had been betrayed by the government.

Friedrich Ebert became the leader of the new government. He was a socialist and member of the Social Democratic Party (SPD). He had the support of some of the army leaders who were afraid of a communist revolution. In 1917 the Bolsheviks had seized power in Russia after a revolution. They turned Russia into a communist country. It was feared that communists would try to do the same in Germany. The German Communist Party (the KPD) was formed in December 1918. In January 1919, a communist group called the **Spartacists** tried to take power in Berlin. This revolution was crushed when Ebert called in the **Freikorps**, bands of ex-soldiers who were violently anti-communist.

SOURCE 1

The proud German army, after victoriously resisting for four years disappeared in a moment. The German government, who had not fought against the enemy, worked to destroy it.

*General Ludendorff, **War Memories**, 1933. He blamed the members of the Reichstag for accepting that Germany had lost the war. He refused to accept this fact.*

The weaknesses of the Weimar Republic.

1 Germany was not used to democracy. The Kaiser had held a lot of power before 1918.	**2** There were lots of small political parties who could not always agree.
3 Voting system of proportional representation made it hard for one party to control the Reichstag (parliament).	**4** President could make laws without the agreement of the Reichstag. EMERGENCY DECREE
5 It was associated with the hated Treaty of Versailles.	**6** Economic problems (reparations; hyper-inflation 1923). SHUT

How the new government was to be run

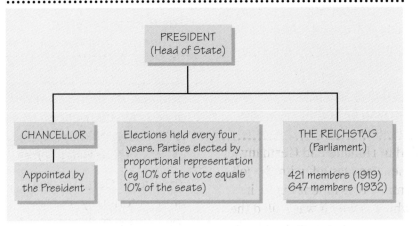

```
                    PRESIDENT
                  (Head of State)
                        |
        +---------------+----------------+
        |               |                |
   CHANCELLOR    Elections held every four    THE REICHSTAG
        |        years. Parties elected by      (Parliament)
   Appointed by  proportional representation
   the President (eg 10% of the vote equals   421 members (1919)
                 10% of the seats)            647 members (1932)
```

Problems facing the Weimar Republic

One of the first actions of the new government was to sign the Treaty of Versailles which ended the war. The treaty was drawn up by the Allies (Britain, France and the USA). Germany was not allowed to take part in any negotiations. Under the treaty, Germany:

- lost 13% of its territory
- had its army reduced to 100,000 men
- was told not to put any troops into the Rhineland
- was ordered to pay **reparations** (war damages) of £6,600 million to the Allies
- was made to sign a war-guilt clause which said that Germany was totally to blame for starting the war.

It was a harsh and humiliating treaty which angered many German people. In 1920, a group of resentful nationalists led by Wolfgang Kapp, tried to take control of the government which was now based in Berlin. The army stood by and did not stop him. He only failed because the Weimar government called on workers to go out on a **general strike**. This brought services to a standstill and made it impossible for Kapp to run the city.

In 1923 the Weimar government said it could no longer afford to pay reparations. The French army then invaded the Ruhr coalfield, intending to take German coal instead of money payments. The German miners, encouraged by their own government, went on strike and refused to mine coal. The miners still had to be paid so the German government just printed more and more money. Paper money soon became worthless and prices went up alarmingly (**hyper-inflation**). Overnight the savings of German people became worthless. The **middle class** was particularly hard hit. The French eventually withdrew their troops, but many Germans had lost all their trust in the Weimar government.

SOURCE 2

With terrible speed we are approaching the complete collapse of the state and of law and order. Prices are rising unchecked. Hardship is growing. Starvation threatens. The government lacks authority and is incapable of overcoming the danger. From the east we are threatened with destruction by communism.

A statement made by Wolfgang Kapp, who tried to overthrow the Weimar Republic, in March 1920.

LUDENDORFF

Erich Ludendorff (1865 –1937) was an important German commander in the First World War. Between August 1916 and November 1918 he and Paul von Hindenburg controlled Germany's war plans. After Germany was defeated he fled to Sweden. In 1919 Ludendorff returned to Munich, supported the nationalists against the Weimar Republic and became a friend of Hitler. From 1924–8 he was a Nazi member of the Reichstag.

Hitler finds an opportunity

In November 1918 Hitler went back to Munich, the capital city of Bavaria (a part of Germany). To his total dismay he found that Bavaria was governed by socialists, under the leadership of a Jew, Kurt Eisner.

In disgust Hitler volunteered for guard duty at a prisoner-of-war camp and left Munich. When he returned, in March 1919, the nationalist Freikorps had overthrown the socialists. The army was keen to keep the socialists out of power. Hitler was made an education officer and told to persuade soldiers not to support communism and socialism.

Hitler joins the German Workers' Party – a political start

Hitler started to visit beer halls in Munich. He would stand on tables and warn people about the evils of socialism and communism. This impressed his officers. He was sent to join an 'enlightenment squad' where he was given lessons in public speaking and trained to attack communist ideas.

In September 1919 Hitler attended a meeting of the German Workers' Party, a small political party which had been set up by Anton Drexler and Dietrich Harrer. Hitler found that the party was poorly organized and realized he had an opportunity to build it up. More than this – he could feed in his own ideas. Hitler began a membership drive and organized big meetings. Many of the new members were ex-soldiers.

Building a political party

By February 1920 the party had been renamed the National Socialist German Workers' Party. This was soon shortened to the Nazi Party. A new party programme, called the 'Twenty Five Points' was drawn up. Amongst other things, this programme said that the party was anti-Jewish and called for changes to make Germany powerful again. It also promised reforms for workers. The word 'socialist' in its title was there in the hope that workers would join it (rather than the SPD or the KPD) and because some party members at the time believed in socialist ideas. Hitler, though, had no real intention of protecting the rights of workers and their trade unions.

In August 1921 the **SA** was set up to protect the party and attack its opponents. Members of the SA wore brown shirts and were also know as Stormtroopers. The SA leader was Ernst Röhm.

SOURCE 3

The trauma of defeat, revolution, and conquest of the state by the hated socialists, the 'national disgrace' of Versailles, a once powerful nation gripped by inflation. By the 1920s, before Hitler came to importance, a longing for a new great leader was common amongst German nationalists.

*I. Kershaw, **Profiles in Power: Hitler**, 1991.*

SOURCE 4

If Hitler meant to enter politics, he had to start somewhere. Here was an organization, small and obscure enough to be turned into something different, a party capable of attracting the masses.

*A. Bullock, writing about why Hitler joined the German Workers' Party in 1919, from **Hitler and Stalin: Parallel Lives**,*

The Munich Putsch

By 1922 Hitler was the leader of the Nazi Party. He was well known in Bavaria as a speaker who had ideas about how to strengthen Germany and destroy its enemies.

The Weimar government was very unpopular, especially in Bavaria. It had accepted the Treaty of Versailles and was blamed for the hyper-inflation. On 8 November 1923 Hitler seized control of a meeting in a Munich beer hall, which had been called by the Bavarian government to discuss the problems of Germany.

Accompanied by armed Stormtroopers, Hitler burst into the beer hall and 'persuaded' the meeting that the time was right to have a national revolution to overthrow the Weimar government. On the morning of 9 November 1923 a force of 3,000 Stormtroopers, with Hitler and General Ludendorff in the lead, marched into the centre of Munich. They were confronted by the police, shots were fired and 17 people were killed. Hitler was injured in the commotion and arrested. What became known as the Munich Putsch had failed.

SOURCE 5

Hitler and others who were put on trial for organizing the Munich Putsch in November 1923. Ludendorff is fifth from the right; Röhm is second from the right.

Hitler in prison – learning from defeat?

Hitler was put on trial for rebelling against the government. At his trial he attacked the Weimar Republic. The trial helped to spread his ideas outside Bavaria and across Germany. Hitler was sentenced to five years in Landsberg prison, but only served nine months. In prison he wrote his autobiography called *Mein Kampf* ('My Struggle') in which he described his beliefs. The first volume was published in 1925 and a second followed in 1926. Another book, called *Zweites Buch* ('Second Book'), was written in 1928 but not published.

In *Mein Kampf*, Hitler explained his beliefs that:

- Germany must conquer new territory in eastern Europe to give the German people living space. He called this **lebensraum**. This would be done by defeating the communist USSR.

- Germany should get revenge for the way it had been treated by the Versailles Treaty.

- All German-speaking people living in Europe should be ruled by one strong leader.

- The Jewish people were the enemies of Germany.

A difficult time for the Nazis

When Hitler was in prison the government banned the Nazi Party and its newspaper. When he was released Hitler realized that he would not gain power by using force. He would have to build up his support and win elections.

In 1923, Gustav Stresemann became the new Chancellor of Germany. He persuaded the French to leave the Ruhr which enabled German industry to start working again. He took measures to end the hyper-inflation and arranged for the USA to lend Germany money. Between 1924 and October 1929 Germany was more prosperous as the economy recovered. More people had jobs than before and working conditions were better. This made the Weimar Republic more popular and removed some of the reasons for people wanting to get rid of it. As a result there was less interest in the Nazi Party during this period. Hitler was also hampered by the fact that he was not allowed to make speeches in public. This ban lasted until 1928.

SOURCE 6

It was now that he began to attend meetings of the Nazi Party. The huge hall, filled with flags, the singing of the National Anthem, the speeches that put into words the hatred that he felt.

Christabel Bielenberg, an English woman living in Germany, explains how her gardener became a Nazi supporter in 1929.

SOURCE 7

When he was released from prison in December 1924, Hitler reformed the Nazi Party. In 1928 the Nazis only had twelve seats in the Reichstag. Hitler concentrated on building up the Party in the country. He looked to the middle classes and the farmers for support. He was helped by a fall in prices at this time, which hit farmers badly. Hitler used rallies, speeches, attacks on his opponents and violence in the streets. In the rural province of Schleswig-Holstein, support for the Nazis increased from 4% of voters in 1928 to 27% in the elections of 1930.

R. Gibson and J. Nichol, Germany, 1985.

The Nazis try to win votes

If the Nazis were going to win elections they needed many more supporters. Hitler tried to appeal to as many different groups in Germany as possible. In the cities Nazi speakers complained about the poor wages of factory workers, to try to get the support of working people. Hitler promised business people he would get rid of the communists. He knew rich people were frightened that a communist revolution would take away their wealth and power. He said he would stop strikes and make sure business people made a lot of money. From 1928 the Nazis promised to help farmers hit by falling prices.

The Nazi's main support came from middle-class people (shopkeepers, skilled workers, civil servants and teachers). Their savings had been made worthless by the hyper-inflation of 1923. They wanted a strong leader to protect them and make Germany powerful again. But still Hitler needed more supporters.

The Wall Street Crash

In October 1929 the world was plunged into an economic depression, following the collapse of the American stock exchange in Wall Street, New York. This became known as the Wall Street Crash. The USA stopped lending money to Germany. Soon German farms and factories were in trouble. Between 1928 and 1932 the number of unemployed people in Germany went up from just under two million to over six million. Most Germans blamed the Weimar Republic. Many people were desperate for someone to bring down unemployment. Hitler was delighted. He knew that desperate people were more likely to listen to his promises to provide Germany with a strong leader and to make it prosperous and powerful again.

WALL STREET CRASH

The Wall Street Crash of 1929 started a world-wide economic crisis. The price of shares on the New York Stock Exchange collapsed. US banks told everyone who had borrowed money that they had to pay it back at once. This affected a lot of people, from families in America to whole countries. The loans stopped. Factories were forced to shut, people lost their jobs. People became desperate. In many countries, including Germany, they voted for extreme political parties.

SOURCE 8

A Nazi election poster, from the early 1930s, following the Wall Street Crash. It reads 'Our last hope: Hitler'. It was designed to appeal to workers faced with unemployment.

Hitler takes power in Germany

The leaders of the Weimar Republic found it very hard to deal with the problems of unemployment which hit Germany after 1929. Between 1930 and the end of 1932 there were three general elections but Germany's problems continued. During this time Hitler toured Germany attacking the Weimar Republic, promising an end to the Versailles Treaty and the high level of unemployment. He also knew that better-off people were scared that there might be a communist revolution and he promised to destroy the communist party or KPD. He spent more time attacking communists than Jews, as he realized he could win more votes this way.

As well as holding meetings, marches and spreading ideas in books and leaflets, uniformed members of the Nazi Party – the Stormtroopers – beat up opponents and fought members of the KPD in the streets. It looked as if law and order was breaking down in Germany.

In March 1932, Hitler stood for the post of President against Field Marshall Hindenburg, who had already been President for seven years. Hindenburg won but Hitler gained a lot of publicity and became a national personality. By November 1932 the Nazis were the biggest party in the Reichstag. In January 1933 President Hindenburg asked Hitler to become **Chancellor**. Hitler gladly accepted. How had he managed to get into power legally?

- People blamed the Weimar Republic for Germany's defeat in the war and the hyper-inflation of 1923.

- Two rival parties – the SPD and KPD – competed for working-class votes. They would not work together against the Nazis.

- Hitler promised to reduce unemployment.

- Leading politicians in the Weimar Republic were more concerned with competing against each other for power than stopping Hitler. Some thought they could use Hitler to get rid of their opponents – then get rid of him. They were wrong!

- No party could get a majority of seats in the Reichstag and so the real power lay with the President.

- President Hindenburg and many powerful Germans did not like the Weimar Republic and did not try to defend it.

SOURCE 9

Hitler himself spoke at sixteen major rallies. Columns of **SS** troops shouting slogans marched through the villages and towns from morning till night. In every market square an SA band or Nazi minstrels played marches for hours on end.

A German eyewitness describes the effort the Nazis put into winning votes, during a ten day period, in the German state of Lippe in January 1933.

Unemployment in Germany (in millions)	
1928	2.5
1930	3.0
1932	5.0
1933	6.0

Unemployment rose sharply in Germany between 1928 and 1933.

Nazi share of the vote in national elections 1928–1933		
Year	Percentage of votes	Number of seats
1928	2	12
1930	18	107
1932 (July)	37	230
1932 (Nov)	33	196
1933	44	288

Between 1928 and 1933 the Nazi's share of the vote increased dramatically.

Hitler increases his power

Hitler called a new general election for March 1933. The Nazis made life hard for their opponents. On 27 February 1933 the Reichstag building mysteriously went up in flames. The Nazis blamed the Communist Party, although the Nazis themselves may have been responsible. Hitler used the fire to get Hindenburg to pass an emergency law which allowed the Nazis to arrest opponents.

In the election the Nazis only won 44% of the votes, which was not enough to give them the overall power needed to pass the laws they wanted. The Nazis, therefore, had to rely on other parties in the Reichstag for support. Hitler was not willing to be controlled. He banned the Communist Party and persuaded the other parties to vote for an **Enabling Act**. This gave Hitler power to rule on his own without consulting anyone else.

Hitler becomes Führer – the supreme leader

After Hitler became Chancellor the SA, under Ernst Röhm, continued to murder opponents and set up special prisons called **concentration camps**. By 1934 the SA had over four million members. Both Hitler and the army thought that Röhm was becoming too powerful. Röhm wanted to join the army and the SA together and become the commander. The army did not like this idea at all. Hitler was afraid that if he did not silence Röhm, the army might act against him. As Hitler could not afford to lose the support of the army he decided to act. On 30 June 1934 Hitler's bodyguard, the SS, murdered Röhm and 70 other SA leaders. This event became known as the Night of the Long Knives. In August 1934 the elderly President Hindenburg died. Hitler now combined the posts of Chancellor and President and declared himself the 'Führer' (leader) of Germany. The army was made to swear an oath of loyalty directly to Hitler. He now had total control.

A German cartoon of 1932 shows the enemies of the Weimar Republic. From left to right: the communist KPD, Nazis, Catholic Centre Party (some of whom tried to work with Hitler) and the socialist SPD. To this could be added the other nationalist groups – the army and many business people.

RÖHM

Ernst Röhm (1887–1934) helped Hitler to start the Nazi Party. He set up the Stormtroopers (SA) as a private Nazi army, to defend their meetings and attack their opponents. In 1925 he went to Bolivia, but returned to Germany in 1930 to help reorganize the SA.

Röhm wanted the SA to replace the German army, but Hitler needed the army's support. Röhm was unpopular, and Hitler began to worry he could not control Röhm or the SA. Röhm was executed, on Hitler's orders (along with other SA leaders), in 1934.

17

How did Nazi rule change everyday life in Germany?

After 1933 the Nazis realized it was important that people accepted the Nazi government and its ideas for running Germany. They knew that many people did not believe in Nazi ideas and in the past had voted for other political parties. The Nazis aimed to change Germany completely but how far did they succeed in this aim?

The Nazis and young people

Hitler thought it was important to make young people grow up supporting the Nazi Party. He therefore established the Hitler Youth Movement to instruct young people in Nazi ideas. From the age of ten boys could join the Young Folk organization and then move up to the Hitler Youth. Girls first joined the Young Maidens, then the League of German Girls. In this way the planned new German Empire (Third Reich) would be sure of the continuing support of its people.

Boys were taught how to march, shoot and act like soldiers. If the Nazis were to succeed in conquering more land in Europe they would need more soldiers. Girls were also encouraged to be fit and healthy but they were taught to become German mothers, having children for Germany. For many children these activities were exciting and gave them an opportunity to make friends and enjoy camping and sporting competitions. At the same time, though, they were taught Nazi beliefs, such as Jews and communists were to blame for the troubles of Germany. They were encouraged to be patriotic and told that the Treaty of Versailles should be torn up. Teachers who did not agree with these ideas were sacked. Jewish teachers were also sacked.

SOURCE 1

Hitler Youth poster from 1933.

SOURCE 2

I just remember how thrilling it was. I loved the constant marching and singing, with flags and bunting everywhere. I wanted to join the League of German Girls but my mother wouldn't let me.

Marga, a German eyewitness, describes how she had felt in 1933, about the Nazi youth organizations.

SOURCE 3

More than a third of German young people were not involved in any Nazi organization. Quite a few who were members only paid membership fees and got out of performing their 'duties' with a doctor's certificate, or a letter from school saying they had learning problems and couldn't afford the time for out of school activities. Some simply didn't show up for duty. Many young people had nothing, or as little as possible, to do with the Nazis.

Kulle, a German eyewitness, remembers life in 1938.

BRAUN

Eva Braun (1912–45) was Hitler's mistress. She met him as she worked for Heinrich Hoffman, Hitler's photographer. She behaved as a Nazi woman was supposed to. She was never seen with Hitler in public and stayed at home, taking no part in politics. Hitler married her on 29 April 1945, the day before they both committed suicide.

Women in Nazi Germany

The Nazis believed that German women should stay in the home and look after children. They believed that they should not work full-time, or get involved in politics. Under the Weimar Republic more women had begun to work, but this trend was stopped after Hitler came to power in 1933. In that year women were forced out of better-paid jobs in the civil service and medicine. In 1936 women who worked as lawyers were also made to give up their careers.

Despite these attempts by the Nazis to make women give up their independence, over four million continued to go out to work. In fact, by the late 1930s, there was a shortage of workers in Germany and more women were needed to work in industry again. It is clear that the Nazis failed to make all women do what they wanted them to.

The Nazis also discouraged women from wearing modern fashions and make-up. In 1935 in one hotel in the Bavarian Alps, signs went up saying: 'Women with red nails and long trousers not admitted.' In Erfurt the police actually stopped women from smoking in public. Some women did as they were told but many others ignored the instructions. It was difficult for the government to do anything about it.

The Nazi government wanted a larger population. Married couples were given loans which did not have to be paid back if they had a large family. Other grants of money were also given to large families and family allowances encouraged more children too. Birth control was discouraged. Between 1933 and 1939 the number of German babies born each year went up.

SOURCE 4

Women do not wish to work in factories or offices. They have no wish to be in politics. A cosy home, a loving husband and a multitude of happy children are closer to their hearts.

Dr Rosten, The ABC of National Socialism, published in the 1930s.

SOURCE 5

Her world is her husband, her family, her children and her home. We do not consider it correct for the woman to interfere in the world of the man. Every child that a woman brings into the world is a battle for the existence of her people.

Hitler in a speech to Nazi women, 1934.

The Nazis and the workers

Before the Nazis came to power many workers had voted for the socialist SPD or the communist KPD. The Nazis realized that they could not rely on the support of many working people. In order to win their support (and thereby control them) the Nazi government used a mixture of force and incentives. They took the following measures:

- Trade unions were banned in 1933 so they could not organize opposition to Hitler.

- The Nazi run German Labour Front (DAF) replaced trade unions.

- In July 1933 the SPD and the KPD were banned.

- The Beauty of Labour (SDA) organization was set up to improve working conditions.

- The Strength Through Joy (KDF) organization gave holidays and cruises for workers who produced a lot of goods.

Under the German Labour Front, wages rose a little but this was nothing in comparison to the huge profits made by the employers. Hitler had no intention of giving power to workers, or annoying the rich industrialists who gave the Nazi Party money. In 1934, the Law for the Organization of National Labour gave employers almost complete power over the lives of their workers.

Under Hitler the workers lost freedom – the leisure and sports activities provided for them were an attempt to disguise their loss of rights. Many workers made the most of these opportunities but did not become Nazi supporters. Although it was difficult and dangerous to oppose the Nazis some workers did resist these changes.

SOURCE 6

5 Mark die Woche musst Du sparen– willst Du im eignen Wagen fahren!

IIIA - 42803

KdF-Wagen: Über Anschaffungspreis und Zahlungsweise erteilen Auskunft alle Betriebswarte und Dienststellen der NS.-Gemeinschaft „Kraft durch Freude" Gau München-Oberbayern

A poster, from 1938, encouraging workers to save up to buy a car. Workers saved huge amounts of money but did not receive any cars from the Nazi government.

SOURCE 7

The aim of the Labour Front is to educate all Germans who are at work to support the Nazi state and to teach them Nazi ways of thinking.

Proclamation to German workers made by the Nazi government in 1933.

The Nazis and the German economy

One of the biggest claims of the Nazi government was that they had saved the German economy and given jobs to people who had been unemployed. When Hitler came to power in 1933 there were six million Germans unemployed. By 1936 this had dropped to 2.5 million; by 1939 it was 300,000. Many working people were grateful and felt that Hitler had achieved these changes for them. This applied to many workers who had not supported the Nazis at first.

The Nazis set up huge work creation schemes to put people back to work. By 1938, 3,000 kilometres of motorways (autobahns) had been built in Germany. A Labour Service was set up which made all men, aged 18–26, work for six months on government work schemes. After 1936 Hitler began to rebuild the armed forces. This, in turn, created many jobs making weapons. A Four Year Plan was set up (1936–40) to prepare Germany for war. Huge amounts of money were spent building factories to make Germany **self-sufficient**. However, Hitler ran out of money to pay for these projects. He did not want to put taxes up which would be unpopular. Only war would allow him to take what he needed from other countries, without having to pay for it.

SOURCE 8

In October 1936 five large crates labelled 'machine parts' – but actually containing brand-new field howitzers [large guns] – were sunk in the harbour. Two more crates were smashed on the wharf and two officials were seriously injured. The **Gestapo** arrested several dockworkers but could not work out who was responsible.

Alma Stobbe, a secret communist trade unionist, describing how some workers in Hamburg hit back at the Nazis. Hamburg was an important port.

SOURCE 9

They often complain about the fact that they earn much less now than in 1929, but at the end of the day they always say: 'At least we have work.' But even now – although they know there is a shortage of workers – they are all scared of losing their jobs. The years of unemployment have not been forgotten.

A secret spy report by the intelligence section of the SS, on how German workers felt in central Germany in 1938.

GÖRING

Hermann Göring (1893–1946) was a fighter pilot in the First World War and was awarded Germany's highest medal for bravery. He joined the Nazis in 1922, but fled to Denmark after the failure of Hitler's attempt to seize power in Munich in 1923.

He returned in 1931 and was elected to the Reichstag in 1932. In 1934 he was put in charge of the Luftwaffe (the German airforce). He founded the Gestapo and led it until 1936.

Göring was put in charge of organizing the Four Year Plan (the German build up to war) and ran the economy until 1943. But he did not prepare Germany for a long war. This (and the failure of the Luftwaffe to protect German cities from Allied air attacks) led to Hitler taking away his powers in 1943. Göring was captured at the end of the war and tried as a war criminal. He was sentenced to death, but committed suicide before the sentence could be carried out.

Nazi attempts to control ideas

The Nazi government tried to control peoples' thoughts and opinions by controlling the information that they were allowed to see and hear. This was done by making sure that only Nazi views were allowed in Germany. As far as the government could control it, people would only hear what the government wanted them to. This is called propaganda. The government stopped people saying, or writing things that the Nazis disagreed with. This is called censorship.

In 1930 Hitler made Joseph Goebbels the head of the Propaganda Division of the Nazi Party.

In 1933, after Hitler came to power, Goebbels became Minister of Popular Enlightenment and Propaganda. He persuaded Hitler to give him control over the press, radio, theatre, films, music, books, painting and sculpture. Goebbels set up the Reich Chamber of Culture to keep an eye on all of these areas. He encouraged students to burn books that did not agree with Nazi views. Over 2,500 writers were banned because they expressed views which the Nazis disagreed with.

The newspapers, too, were not allowed to print stories which the Nazis were unhappy with. All stories had to support the government and make people think that Hitler was right in the things he did and said. People were often told things that were untrue in order to make them believe in Hitler.

Films were also used to put over the Nazi view of world events and history. Some films attacked the people the Nazis hated. One of the most famous was 'The Eternal Jew', which compared Jewish people to rats and claimed that Jews were the enemy of the German people. This film was shown throughout Germany and – during the Second World War – in those countries occupied by the Germans.

Goebbels also set up spectacular events to astonish people with their sound and colour and persuade them that it was right to be a Nazi. Vast rallies were held at Nuremberg which were attended by thousands of people. These were dramatic occasions with marches and music and great meetings held at night with searchlights sweeping across the sky.

SOURCE 10

Nazi posters were dramatic and designed to spread a message in an eye-catching way. This one shows a Nazi worker smashing international banks which Germany owed money to.

SOURCE 11

A Nazi Party rally in the 1930s.

SOURCE 12

Hitler himself was to speak at an open air rally. It was held appropriately – as Peter pointed out – in Hamburg's zoo.
Peter survived the community singing, the rolling of drums, the National and Party anthems. Then Hitler began to speak. My ears were hardly used to his Austrian accent when I was marched out of the enclosure by a disgusted Peter. He made one of his rare political pronouncements: 'You may think that the Germans are political idiots, and you may be right, but I can assure you that they won't be so stupid as to fall for that clown.'

Christabel Bielenberg describes the reaction of her husband to a Nazi Party propaganda rally.

SOURCE 13

It is not enough for people to accept our rule. We want to work on people until they surrender to us. Until they choose to believe in what is happening in Germany.

Goebbels, in 1933, explaining how he wanted to control people's ideas until they believed in him and in Nazism.

GOEBBELS

Paul Joseph Goebbels (1897–1945) was a journalist who joined the Nazis in 1924 and was made a district organizer in 1926. In 1928 he began to organize Nazi propaganda, setting up the Nazi paper, *Der Angriff* (*the Attack*). When Hitler came to power he took control of news and culture and, after 1938, led attacks on Jews. He stayed with Hitler to the end, committing suicide (with his wife and six children) on 1 May 1945.

Nazi attitudes towards Jewish people

When Hitler joined the German Workers' Party in 1919 he found many members were against the Jews. There were about 500,000 German Jews. Many Jews had given their lives for Germany in the First World War. Although the Jews had done nothing to deserve this prejudice, many German nationalists blamed them for all the problems facing Germany. Why they felt this way is not alway clear but there seem to have been a number of factors which caused them to pick on innocent Jewish people:

- Jewish people belonged to a different religion.

- Some Jews, especially in the Austro-Hungarian Empire, looked and spoke differently to Germans.

- Some Jewish people were successful and wealthy and this made other people jealous of them. Many Jews were doctors, lawyers and writers.

- The founder of communism – Karl Marx – had been a Jew and he was hated by nationalists because he thought a person's class was more important than the country he or she belonged to.

- Ever since the Middle Ages there had been a tradition in Europe of blaming Jews for problems that they had nothing to do with.

Hitler's dislike of the Jews dated back to his days living as a tramp in Vienna. In his early speeches he blamed Jews for Germany's problems and spoke vaguely about getting rid of them.

Persecution of the Jews in the 1930s

After they came to power in 1933, the Nazis began to persecute the Jews. The level of persecution built up gradually over the years.

In 1933 the SA celebrated Hitler becoming Chancellor by beating up Jewish people in the street. On 1 April 1933, Hitler ordered a boycott of Jewish shops, lawyers and doctors. Banners were put up in the street telling people not to buy from Jewish shopkeepers; members of the SA were positioned outside Jewish shops to stop people going in.

After this other ways were used to force the Jews out of German life. Jews were excluded from parks, swimming pools, restaurants and public buildings. They were banned from working in the civil service and could no longer inherit land.

SOURCE **14**

A Nazi election poster from 1932. It reads: 'We farmers are clearing out the muck'. It shows the people the Nazis hated most – Jews, communists and socialists.

In September 1935 Hitler felt confident enough to pass the Nuremberg Laws. Under these laws Jews lost their German citizenship and could no longer vote in elections. Marriages between Jews and non-Jews were made illegal. In 1936 the Olympic Games were held in Berlin. Persecution of the Jews was halted – Hitler knew the many visitors to Berlin from abroad would be horrified if they happened to witness the Jewish people being treated so disgracefully.

Kristallnacht – the Night of Broken Glass

By 1938 Hitler was secure in his control of Germany and was convinced that other countries dare not take action against him. Goebbels was therefore allowed to organize an attack on Jewish property. On the night of 9–10 November 1938, thousands of Jewish shop windows were smashed and synagogues burned down. It was a callous attack on a whole community. The Nazis called the event 'Kristallnacht' ('Crystal Night'), after the sound of windows breaking. No ordinary German person had any idea of where all of this was leading (see Unit 6). Some Germans ignored Hitler's actions against the Jews because he had reduced unemployment and rejected the Treaty of Versailles. Those who disliked his actions were too frightened to speak out. Other countries were shocked at his actions.

SOURCE 15

An older man stared out at a devastated shoe store and remarked so loudly that everyone could hear him: 'Once upon a time looters were shot; now the police protect them. That's what Germany's come to. The country we risked our lives for!'

An eyewitness report of the reaction of a German bus passenger to seeing the damage caused to Jewish shops by the Nazis on 'Kristallnacht' (9–10 November 1938).

SOURCE 16

Their first victim was Philipp, a delicate, very pale boy of twelve. Four Hitler Youths from the middle school all considerably stronger than Philipp attacked him and beat him brutally with their fists and belts. When a few classmates and I came running to his aid, the bullies beat a hasty retreat. One of them shouted to us: 'If Hitler comes to power today, we'll string them all up, the Jewish swine!'

Bernt Engelmann, an eye witness, describing a Nazi attack on a Jewish schoolboy in May 1932.

STREICHER

Julius Streicher (1885–1946) was a Nazi journalist and politician. He started an anti–Jewish campaign in 1919 and took part in Hitler's attempt to seize power in Munich in 1923.

From 1923–45 he was editor of the newspaper *Der Sturmer*. This printed fictional stories designed to make Germans hate and fear the Jews. He tried to get children to read the paper, too. Hitler put him in charge of the area of Germany called Franconia. He was captured at the end of the war and tried as a war criminal. He was found guilty and hanged.

Hitler and the World – Why was there another war in 1939?

Hitler came to power in 1933. By 1939 he had led Germany into the Second World War. Why did this terrible war break out? Before we can try to answer this large question we need to look at the events of the 1930s. Historians ask a number of questions when looking at the evidence about these events. These questions are:

- What were Hitler's aims when he took power in Germany?
- How did the German people feel about the things that he did in the 1930s, which affected Germany's relationship with other European countries?
- Why did other countries not stop him?
- Did he carefully plan the things he did in the 1930s, or did he grab any opportunities to make Germany more powerful, without having really planned them?
- Why was it the German attack on Poland on 1 September 1939 which finally led to the Second World War?

Hitler and the Treaty of Versailles

Hitler, like many Germans, hated the way Germany had been punished by the Treaty of Versailles in 1919. There were a number of things about the treaty which he was determined to change:

- Germany had lost land and some Germans had been forced to live in new countries set up by the Treaty of Versailles, such as Poland and Czechoslovakia. Germany had been ordered not to unite with Austria to make one large German-speaking country. Hitler wanted to have all Germans in Europe living under one leader.
- Germany had been forced to reduce her armed forces. Hitler wanted to make Germany a powerful country again.
- Germany had lost its colonies and Hitler wanted more 'living space' (lebensraum) for Germans to live in. He wanted more land in Europe to get this.
- Germany had been forced to pay reparations (war damages) which Hitler was determined to stop.

SOURCE 1

1 We demand the bringing together of all Germans in a greater Germany.

2 We demand equal status for Germany compared to other nations and the end of the Treaty of Versailles.

3 We demand land and property to provide food for our nation and new areas for our population to settle in.

*From the **Twenty-Five Points**. This was the official programme of the Nazi Party, first announced by Hitler on 24 February 1920.*

SOURCE 2

Germany is determined to concentrate all its forces on providing our nation with enough living space. Such space can only be found in the east [of Europe].

*Adolf Hitler, writing in his **Second Book**, 1928.*

Hitler triumphantly salutes the crowd in Vienna, Austria, in 1938.

Hitler tears up the Treaty of Versailles

After 1933 Hitler began to free Germany from the restrictions placed on the country after the First World War. He left the League of Nations in 1933 because other countries would not reduce their own weapons and would not allow Germany to **rearm**. In 1935 he announced that Germany had an air force, which was forbidden by the Treaty of Versailles. A week later, when no other country had made a move to stop him, Hitler reintroduced **conscription** aimed at making the German army 550,000 strong. This also broke the treaty.

In 1936 German troops re-entered the Rhineland. The Treaty of Versailles said that no German soldiers should be stationed in this area which bordered north-eastern France. Hitler gave his soldiers orders to retreat if they were opposed but the French and British did nothing to stop him. Many people in these countries thought Germany had been too harshly treated and had a right to put soldiers in German territory. Also, they were unwilling to risk a war over something which did not seem important. Many Germans supported what Hitler had done. That same year he formed an alliance with Italy (the Rome-Berlin Axis). In March 1938 he went a lot further and openly defied the Treaty of Versailles by uniting Germany and Austria. This was called the *Anschluss*. One month later, 99.75% of Austrians voted that they agreed with this action.

This giant [Russia] will start to fall and then our hour will come. Then we must get ourselves land to last 100 years. Let's hope we're ready then and that the Führer is still alive so that action will be taken.

Goebbels describing Hitler's ideas in his diary, 9 June 1936.

MUSSOLINI

Benito Mussolini (1883–1945) started the Italian Fascist Party in 1919. He wanted to make it the only party in Italy. In 1922 the Fascists marched on Rome. Mussolini was made prime minister. During the 1930s Mussolini was suspicious of Hitler, but became his ally in 1936. But Italy suffered defeats in the war. Mussolini was executed by Italian resistance fighters in 1945.

The Czech and Polish crises – Steps to war?

After the union with Austria, the western part of the neighbouring country of Czechoslovakia (the Sudetenland) was surrounded on three sides by German territory. Three million Germans lived in this area. Hitler now demanded that the Sudetenland should become part of Germany. The Czech government would not agree to this demand and Hitler threatened to invade. France was an ally of Czechoslovakia but would not act without the support of Britain.

Neville Chamberlain, the British Prime Minister, adopted a policy of **appeasement**. He said that the British people did not want to go to war over 'a quarrel in a faraway country'. He thought that the Germans in the Sudetenland should be allowed to unite with Germany and that Hitler would make no more demands for territory after this.

Chamberlain flew to Germany to speak to Hitler. On 30 September 1938, at a conference in Munich, Britain, France and Italy agreed that Hitler should take the Sudetenland. The Czechs were forced to accept this agreement. Hitler said he would not demand anymore territory and Chamberlain returned to Britain saying it was 'peace in our time'.

In March 1939, Hitler broke his promise and invaded the rest of Czechoslovakia.

This time, though, he could not claim that he was bringing Germans back into Germany or that he was correcting something done to Germany by the Treaty of Versailles. Then his attention turned to Poland, which had been given German land by the Treaty of Versailles. Britain now decided that Hitler could not be trusted and promised to help Poland if it was attacked. In August 1939 Hitler signed a friendship treaty with the USSR, which opened the way for a German attack on Poland without the Soviets opposing Germany. Many people were shocked that the Nazis and the USSR had made such a pact.

The German government spread false stories about Poles attacking German people and threatening Germany itself. This was to prepare the German people for the outbreak of war. On 1 September 1939 Germany invaded Poland. This time, though, Hitler had gone too far. On 3 September, Britain and France declared war on Germany. The Second World War had started.

SOURCE 8

Hitler enters the Sudetenland in October 1938. He is greeted by wildly cheering crowds of Sudeten Germans.

SOURCE 9

Warsaw Threatens Bombardment – Proof of Polish Greed for Power.

German Families Escape from Polish Monsters.

Three German Passenger Planes Shot at by Poles.

Flames Destroy German Farmhouses in Polish Territory.

German newspaper headlines in August 1939.

SOURCE 10

I rode into town. No crowds had gathered. We saw no trace of rejoicing, certainly none of the wild enthusiasm that Germans had shown when war broke out before in August 1914. Here and there small groups of people clustered around the news-stands talking quietly, depressed and anxious.

Bernt Engelmann, a German eyewitness, in September 1939.

BENES

Eduard Benes (1884–1948) became president of Czechoslovakia in 1935. He tried to give in to the demands of the Sudeten Germans, but he could not satisfy the Nazis. When the Nazis seized the Sudetenland the French and British did nothing to help. Benes resigned and left the country. He returned in April 1940, but Czechoslovakia was now in the hands of the USSR. He resigned in 1948, in protest at the communist takeover of his country.

Hitler – a man with a plan?

Some historians think Hitler had a clear plan of what he wanted to do in the 1930s. It was a plan leading to a full-scale war across Europe. He had made it clear what his aims were and when he came to power he followed these aims. Other historians think he simply grabbed opportunities to make Germany stronger whenever he could. He was a gambler who took risks and eventually pushed too far and ended up with a war he did not want against Britain and France. They go on to suggest that there were lots of reasons why he acted the way he did and also that lots of other people carry a responsibility for what eventually happened.

Some of these different points of view, or **interpretations**, are described here. You need to look at these interpretations and what you have found out so far in order to make up your own mind about Hitler's intentions.

> *Everything I do is directed against the U.S.S.R. If those in the West are too stupid and blind to understand this, then I shall be forced to come to an agreement with the U.S.S.R. to beat the West and then turn with all my force against the U.S.S.R.*

Adolf Hitler in 1939.

TWO VIEWS OF HITLER

1 A Man With a Plan

Clear aims to conquer empires in 'the East' and control Europe.

Builds up armed forces.

Builds strong war economy.

Unites Germans of Austria and Sudetenland.

Marches east as he said he would. Next: the World?!

2 A Man Without a Plan

Vague plans and no clear ideas.

Carried on ideas put forward by Kaiser and army.

Cautious about annoying other countries at first.

Economy in trouble by 1936, cannot afford big military build-up.

Has to impress Germans, Nazi Party, Army ...

Captures land to take resources he cannot afford to buy

Gambles on other countries letting him take land. Does not want a big war.

Plunges into a war with Britain and France by mistake!

SOURCE 11

From late 1937 onwards it was clear that Hitler was set on taking over central Europe. By 1938 the time had come for Hitler to put into practice his plan to add living space [Lebensraum] to Germany.

*H. Mills, **Twentieth Century World History in Focus**, 1984.*

SOURCE 12

In 1939 Hitler demanded territory from Poland. This time Britain and France said they would stand by the Poles if Germany attacked. Hitler, perhaps convinced by the events of the previous years that they would not, invaded when the Poles refused to give him the land.

*P. Shuter and T. Lewis, **Skills in History: The Twentieth Century**, 1989.*

SOURCE 13

The power of Germany was directed by Adolf Hitler. The broad decisions were decided in all cases by Hitler. On major issues of policy the Führer did what he wanted.

*G. Weinberg, **The Foreign Policy of Hitler's Germany**, 1980.*

SOURCE 14

The only plan was the friendship with Britain. By the mid 1930s that had failed and any 'basic plan' was in tatters – resulting by 1939 in friendship with the enemy [the USSR] and war with the would-be 'friend' [Britain].

*I, Kershaw, **The Nazi Dictatorship**, 1989.*

SOURCE 15

How important was Adolf Hitler to the outbreak of the Second World War? Did he control events, or was he swept along by them? There were some factors in world history that were much more powerful than any one person. Some people in many countries were opposed to the Treaty of Versailles. Another 'impersonal factor' was the horror of war that many people felt. Yet another was the world slump and the massive unemployment. During the 1930s these, and other factors combined in a pattern that led to war in 1939.

*J. Scott, **The World Since 1914**, 1989.*

SOURCE 16

Far from wanting war, a general war was the last thing he [Hitler] wanted. He wanted total victory without total war. One thing he did not plan was the great war blamed on him.

*A. J .P. Taylor, **Origins of the Second World War**, 1961.*

HITLER AND THE USA

Hitler's attitude to the USA shows how he sometimes failed to make long-term plans. He ignored the USA in the early 1920s, except for criticizing its support for the Treaty of Versailles. He vaguely considered an alliance, but decided that the USA was a weak and racially inferior country.

By 1941 he had come to realize that the USA was more powerful than he had thought, he feared they might join the war against him. He went to war with the USA with no clear ideas as to how he could win.

31

Why did Germany lose the Second World War?

On 1 September 1939 Germany invaded Poland. On 3 September Britain and France declared war on Germany – the Second World War had begun. To begin with the war went very well for the Germans. They captured country after country and seemed to be unbeatable. Yet by 1945 they were beaten and Germany was totally crushed. Why did Germany lose the Second World War? Before answering this question historians ask a number of other questions first:

- Why was Germany so successful in the first part of the war?
- When and why did these successes turn to failures?
- How did the war affect the German people and life in Germany?

We will look at each of these questions in turn and then examine different interpretations about why Germany lost.

Why was Germany so successful in the first part of the war?

The Poles fought bravely against the Germans but were no match for the well equipped German armies who used a new method of fighting called **blitzkrieg** (lightning war):

- The German air force (the Luftwaffe) pounded enemy factories, roads, railways, airfields and defences.
- Huge numbers of fast and powerful tanks smashed through enemy defences on the ground.
- Troops in lorries followed, killing any enemy troops who had been cut off by the fast advance of the tanks and taking control of the countryside. It was possible to take up to 100 km of territory a day using the blitzkrieg method.

The Poles were not equipped or trained to strike back. The Polish cavalry was no match for the German tanks. The Polish capital, Warsaw, was heavily bombed. Meanwhile, Germany's new ally, the USSR, invaded Poland from the east on 17 September. Within a month Poland had been defeated.

In April 1940 the Germans invaded Denmark and Norway. In May 1940 German armies burst into France, Belgium and the Netherlands.

SOURCE 1

[On 10 May 1940] the Germans launched a blitzkrieg attack. German tanks rolled swiftly across Holland and Belgium. Other troops attacked France through the Ardennes avoiding the **Maginot Line**. Holland surrendered within five days. By the tenth day the Germans had reached the Channel. The Germans were so successful partly because the Allies were not really ready for war.

Christopher Culpin, Making History: World History from 1914 to the Present Day, 1984.

SOURCE 2

[By 26 May] British troops were trapped on the beaches of Dunkirk. The rescue of this defeated army was remarkable. While ships of the Royal Navy stood offshore, tugboats, pleasure steamers and river launches picked up the men. Hitler now had control of the Channel coast.

M.N. Duffy, The Twentieth Century, 1983.

The French had hoped that their defences – the Maginot Line – would hold back the Germans but it did not stretch as far as the Belgian border and the Germans went round it! Britain and France were not ready for the new fast tank war. By 4 June the British had evacuated their army from France at the port of Dunkirk. On 22 June 1940 France surrendered.

During the summer of 1940 the Germans had their first setback. The Luftwaffe failed to beat the British airforce in the Battle of Britain. Hitler's plan to invade Britain ('Operation Sealion') was abandoned. Instead the Luftwaffe began to bomb British cities (the **blitz**). In November 1940, Hungary, Romania and Slovakia (all that was left of Czechoslovakia) became official allies of Germany who appeared to have won the war.

In March 1941, a German army (the *Afrika Korps*) captured large areas of North Africa from British troops. In April, Yugoslavia and Greece were attacked and quickly defeated by the Germans. They went on to take Crete using **paratroops** to surprise the British. In June 1941 Hitler invaded the USSR – his ally since 1939. At first the blitzkrieg had the same rapid results. Huge areas of the western USSR were captured and millions of Soviet soldiers surrendered to the Germans. Like the British and French, the Soviets were not ready for this new type of warfare. They were poorly organized and taken by surprise. By the early winter of 1941, the German army had almost reached the Soviet capital, Moscow.

Europe and North Africa at the end of 1941.

GUDERIAN

Heinz Guderian (1888–1954) a German general and tank commander, helped plan blitzkrieg. Hitler was impressed and gave him command of tank armies in Poland and France. He was dismissed from the army for retreating from a Russian attack in 1942.

33

When and why did Germany's successes turn to failure and defeat?

At the end of 1941 Germany seemed unbeatable. But already Hitler's plans had begun to go wrong. He had intended to defeat Britain before he turned on the USSR, but he failed to do this. This meant that when he attacked the USSR he was fighting in both eastern Europe and western Europe. He was convinced that Britain could do him no harm. But, in 1944, Britain would be used as a base from which the Allies invaded Europe to free the countries Germany had conquered. Germany's problems were starting.

The turning point: Germany attacks the USSR

When Hitler turned on the USSR he was taking on a gigantic nation which was to be more than a match for him. This was because:

- The USSR was a huge country and difficult to control.
- The Germans were not equipped well enough to survive the harsh winters of the USSR.
- The Germans treated the Soviet people badly and were soon hated. In many places resistance fighters fought back against the Germans.
- Many Soviet factories, making large numbers of tanks and planes, were beyond the reach of the German army.
- The Soviet army was very big and could bring in experienced troops from Asia to make up for the millions captured and killed by the Germans.
- The Soviet army learned from its early mistakes and struck back at the Germans.

In the winter of 1941 the Soviet army stopped the Germans before they could capture Moscow. Fresh Soviet soldiers caused terrible casualties to the Germans, who were already suffering from the cold. In December, Hitler declared war on the USA, a country enormously more powerful than Germany. The war was turning into a long and bloody one, which Germany was simply not prepared for. Hitler had gambled on a short war.

In 1942 the Germans advanced again – this time attempting to capture the Soviet oilfields – but in the winter of 1942–3 they were defeated at the battle of Stalingrad. Also in 1942, the British began to bomb German cities and, in October, defeated the Germans in North Africa at the battle of El Alamein.

SOURCE 3

I cannot avoid the conclusion that the Soviet army is killing more enemy soldiers and destroying more enemy equipment than the rest of the Allies put together.

President Roosevelt of the USA, speaking in 1943.

SOURCE 4

In June 1941 the Germans stupidly attacked the USSR. Hitler underrated the USSR and by 1942 the Germans were overstretched and suffering enormous losses. The USA was now in the war. With the huge resources of the USA the chances of an Allied defeat were now small.

H. Mills, Twentieth Century World History in Focus, 1984.

SOURCE 5

By the beginning of November each regiment had lost about 400 men to frostbite. The tanks could barely move; to get them started we had to light fires under the oil pans. Our weapons jammed in the cold.

The German General, Heinz Guderian, remembers the winter of 1941 in the USSR.

The beginning of the end for Germany

In May 1943 the German and Italian armies, fighting the Allies in North Africa, surrendered. In July the Allies invaded Sicily. Meanwhile the Soviet army – equipped with huge numbers of new tanks – smashed the Germans at the battle of Kursk in July and August. Germany never recovered.

Throughout 1944 Germany was slowly overwhelmed by the sheer number of its enemies fighting in different parts of Europe. The Soviet army advanced into Romania, Poland and Bulgaria. On 6 June 1944 ('D-Day') the Allies invaded France, from Britain. Germany was unable to replace the men and machines destroyed in the fighting. German cities were being destroyed by air raids. In April 1945 Hitler committed suicide and the German surrender followed in May.

A German poster from 1943. It was written in Russian and claimed that Nazi Germany was winning the Second World War.

Hitler declares war on USA – an enormously powerful country.

Britain still in the war and a threat to Hitler in Western Europe.

Hitler decides on a quick war to defeat the communist USSR.

**1941
The Turning Point**

Germans not ready for a long war as USSR fights back.

Massive Soviet losses but USSR not quickly beaten!

ROOSEVELT

Franklin D. Roosevelt (1882–1945) was elected to the US Senate in 1910. He fell ill with polio in 1921, but stayed in politics. He was elected governor of New York in 1928 and 1930 and president of the USA in 1932. He helped the USA to cope with the economic problems caused by the Wall Street Crash. He led the USA in the war against both Germany and Japan.

The Home Front in Germany

The Second World War was a total war which involved civilians as well as soldiers. The lives of German civilians were greatly affected by the war:

- Many worked in industries making weapons for the war.

- They suffered shortages of food as the war made it hard for Germany to trade with other countries.

- Allied bombing raids increased as the war went on.

- In 1944–45 many became refugees as they were forced to flee from the fighting.

How did the war affect German workers and industry?

Hitler was not prepared for fighting a long war. His Four Year Plan to prepare Germany for war had failed to make the country ready for a war that lasted for almost six years. Fighting both the USSR and the USA, after 1941, meant that Germany was struggling with two mighty nations. German industry was not strong enough to cope with such a struggle. As the war dragged on Germany began to run out of oil for its tanks and planes and other vital resources to keep it going. It became harder to get supplies from other countries. Food had to be rationed as Germany could not produce enough for its people. Many people bought food illegally on the **black market**.

Many of the worst jobs were done by foreign workers from occupied countries, who were forced to work in Germany; by September 1944 they numbered seven and a half million. Many came from eastern Europe. Two million prisoners-of-war were also forced to work in factories, mines and on farms. As the war dragged on, German workers, too, were forced to work long hours. The Nazis had to employ women in great numbers in the factories – even though they had always disapproved of women workers. Things were now desperate and the Nazis had no choice.

SOURCE 7

When I finally got home I could have fallen asleep standing up. Luckily we didn't have air-raids that first year, or I would have collapsed. Many women in our factory did later on. They couldn't take the pace and that wasn't surprising when you think how little food we ate.

Frau Neuber, a German eyewitness, recalls life as a woman war-worker in 1940.

SOURCE 8

Are the German people determined to work 10,12, and if necessary, 14 and 16 hours a day and to give all you have for victory? Do you want total war? This nation is ready for anything!

From a speech by Joseph Goebbels, made in 1943.

SOURCE 9

Germany will soon run out of fuel. In Berlin they're already taking in the harvest with horses. They're growing wheat, potatoes and cabbages right in the middle of the capital of Germany.

Major von Elken, in July 1943. The problems Germany faced after Allied attacks made it difficult to buy oil from Romania.

How did bombing affect the lives of German people?

From 1942 the British and Americans began to bomb German cities heavily. Thousands of German civilians were killed and towns and cities were wrecked. Despite this, the German people learnt to cope with the destruction and loss of life. Until the summer of 1944, many German industries managed to increase the amount of goods they were making, even though factories had been damaged by the Allied bombing. After this Germany was unable to make up for the damage done but, by then, the war was almost lost anyway. The bombing alone, however, was not enough to beat Germany.

Towards the end of the war, life in German cities was very difficult as a result of the bombing and food shortages. Street gangs with Hollywood names like the 'Navahoes' and 'Raving Dudes' became a problem to the authorities. As early as 1942, over 700 were arrested; their ringleaders were hanged. In 1944 the German police in Cologne were attacked by gangs made up of young people, deserters from the German army, escaped Allied prisoners-of-war and foreign workers.

SOURCE 10

In the summer of 1943 we decided that the children should not go through another winter in Berlin. Despite the black market, the food situation got worse month by month. We also knew that longer nights would bring renewed British bombing raids. The bombs fell on Nazis and anti-Nazis, on women and children, works of art, dogs and pet canaries. The British were thoughtless.

Christabel Bielenberg, an English eyewitness, married to a German, remembers life in Berlin.

SPEER

Albert Speer (1905–81) was a German Nazi leader and writer. He was made the official architect of the Nazi Party and designed many impressive official buildings, including the huge stadium in Nuremberg which was used for Nazi rallies.

Speer was an efficient organizer. In 1942 Hitler made him Minister for Armaments. He was responsible for the use of slave labour to build roads and lines of defence.

At the end of the war he was captured and tried. He was imprisoned, but he was later released.

SOURCE 11

Women clear rubble in bombed Berlin.

Opposition to Hitler in Germany

Many Germans did not support Hitler. There were attempts on Hitler's life in 1943 and 1944. Four main groups opposed the Nazis:

The Church

A number of German Christians peacefully opposed Hitler. When the Nazis began to kill disabled people in 1939, they were openly condemned by the Bishop of Munster and other Christians. This criticism was enough to stop the killings. Christians were imprisoned for working against the Nazis and some, such as Dietrich Bonhoeffer, were executed.

Students

A group of Munich students called the 'White Rose' movement condemned the Nazis for their violence and cruelty and tried to encourage other students to oppose Hitler. The leaders, Hans and Sophie Scholl, were rounded up by the Gestapo and executed in 1943.

Communists and socialists

Members of the KPD and SPD secretly helped to smuggle Jews out of Germany and encouraged workers to oppose the way the Nazis ran industry, although this was very hard to do.

Members of the army

The army could have easily overthrown Hitler. In 1938 a group of officers planned a revolt. They feared Hitler would cause a war which Germany would lose. The revolt was abandoned because Hitler's popularity increased when Germany took the Sudetenland. Between 1939 and 1942 it was difficult to oppose Hitler as Germany was winning the war. Things changed in 1943, after the defeat of the German army at Stalingrad. A number of officers planned to kill Hitler. A bomb was placed in Hitler's plane but it failed to explode. The Gestapo began a campaign to root out the opposition and arrests were made. Despite this, on 20 July 1944, a bomb was placed in Hitler's headquarters inside a briefcase. The bomb went off but Hitler escaped serious injury. The army officers responsible for placing the bomb were arrested and executed.

SOURCE 12

I swear by God this holy oath: I will give complete obedience to the Führer of the German Reich and People, Adolf Hitler, the Supreme Commander of the Armed Forces and will be ready, as a brave soldier, to risk my life for this oath.

The oath of loyalty which every German soldier made from August 1934 onwards.

SOURCE 13

Both honour and duty demand that we should do our best to bring about the downfall of Hitler to save Germany and Europe from barbarism.

Henning von Tresckow, a senior German army officer, in 1939.

SOURCE 14

From the ceiling hung six big hooks. In one corner stood a movie camera, for Hitler wanted to see and hear how his enemies died. 'I want them to be hung up like butcher's meat'. Those were his words.

Eyewitness report of how those who opposed Hitler, in 1944, were killed.

Weaknesses of the opposition

Despite the fact that there were people willing to oppose Hitler they all failed. The opposition groups were divided and did not have the same aims. They also did not know how to go about the job properly. Even though many Germans despised the Nazis, they tended to keep quiet when the war was going well for Germany. Above all, people were terrified of what might happen to them if they were found out by the Gestapo.

SOURCE 15

First Hitler failed to capture the British armies stranded at Dunkirk. Second he failed to press home his advantages in the Battle of Britain. Third he decided to invade the USSR. Then he declared war on the USA.

B. Catchpole, A Map History of the Modern World, 1982.

SOURCE 16

It was the massive production of the USA that made victory certain in the end. Factories in Britain and the USSR worked long and hard but many were damaged by German attacks and they were short of raw materials and workers. In the USA there was plenty of everything and no war damage.

J. Scott, The World Since 1914, 1989.

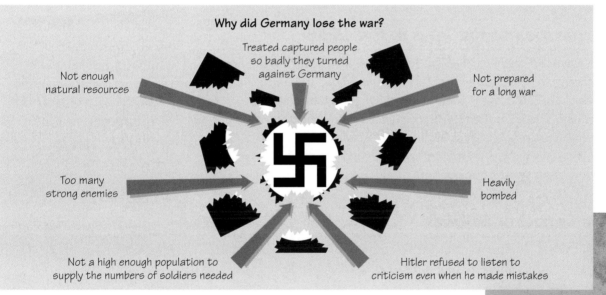

Why did Germany lose the war?

- Treated captured people so badly they turned against Germany
- Not enough natural resources
- Not prepared for a long war
- Too many strong enemies
- Heavily bombed
- Not a high enough population to supply the numbers of soldiers needed
- Hitler refused to listen to criticism even when he made mistakes

Germany lost the war for a variety of reasons.

BONHOEFFER

Dietrich Bonhoeffer (1906–45) was a German Christian church leader and writer. He studied at several universities and believed that all Christians should work together, no matter what church they belonged to. After 1933 he worked against the Nazis, seeing where their ideas were leading them.

When the Nazis came to power Bonhoeffer worked for the German resistance. He was arrested by the Gestapo in April 1943 and imprisoned. He was executed on 9 April 1945, at Flossenberg concentration camp.

What was the 'Final Solution'?

During the Second World War the Nazis were responsible for the killing of approximately six million people, murdered simply because they were Jewish. The Nazis believed they were not truly human and should be destroyed. The Nazis called this the **'Final Solution'** to what they saw as the Jewish problem. This mass extermination of Jewish people is known as the Holocaust. Hitler had long promised to get rid of all Jews in Europe, but the questions we must think about are:

- Had the 'Final Solution' been his aim before the war?
- How and why did the Nazi treatment of the Jews change during the war?

Persecution of the Jews in the 1930s

The ways the Nazis treated the Jews grew worse during the late 1930s. As well as taking away their rights, under the Nuremberg Laws of 1935, the Nazis tried to force Jews to leave German territory. The SS, under Heinrich Himmler, and the police were given the job of getting rid of the Jews. Between 1933 and 1939, 500,000 Jews left German territory. They were forced to leave most of their possessions behind.

The impact of the war

With the start of the war the Nazi treatment of the Jews began to get worse. This happened for a number of reasons:

- It was more difficult to force Jews to emigrate.
- It did not matter what foreign countries thought of Germany any more.
- Hitler had great successes in the war and felt no one could stop him. He now believed he had the opportunity to destroy the Jews of Europe.
- The conquest of Poland in 1939 had brought three million more Jews under Nazi control. The Nazis had to decide what to do about this.

Step by step the Nazis began to develop a more brutal plan.

SOURCE 1

The Jew must get out of Germany, yes out of the whole of Europe. That will take some time yet, but will happen.

Hitler to Goebbels, November 1937.

SOURCE 2

If war comes, the result would not be the world becoming communist and the victory of the Jews but the destruction of the Jewish race.

Adolf Hitler, 30 January 1939.

SOURCE 3

I have always been mocked as a prophet. Of those who laughed then, there are countless numbers who are no longer laughing and those who are still laughing now, will perhaps not be doing it in the time to come.

Adolf Hitler, November 1942, referring to his speech of January 1939.

Nazi treatment of the Jews starts to change

- From 1939 Jews in Poland were forced to move into cities by Special Action Squads of the SS (**Einsatzgruppen**).

- In these cities they were forced to live in **ghettoes**, overcrowded areas which were cut off from non-Jews.

- By 1941 Jews in the ghettoes were facing disease and starvation.

- Some members of the SS Security Police began to consider ways to get rid of large numbers of Jewish people. Between 1939 and 1941 the SS had gained experience gassing mentally and physically disabled people in Germany (the T4 Programme).

The invasion of the USSR – the start of a new approach

In 1941 the German army invaded the USSR. For Hitler this attack was an opportunity to slaughter once and for all both communists and Jews – people he hated. On top of this, there were large numbers of Jews living in the parts of the western USSR captured by the German army. Himmler, the SS commander, sent four Einsatzgruppen, made up of 3,000 men into the USSR. They had been specially trained by his deputy, Reinhard Heydrich, to kill Jews.

By the end of 1941 500,000 Soviet Jews had been shot and buried in mass graves near their homes. Some SS groups experimented in killing Jews in 'gas-vans'. The SS began to discuss ways of killing even more Jews and their plans included more than just the Soviet Jews. Now they were discussing the lives of every Jewish person living under Nazi control in the whole of Europe. A new, larger plan of mass murder had started.

DE EEUWIGE JOOD

OOK U MOET DEZE FILM ZIEN!
EEN DOCUMENTAIRE FILM OVER HET WERELD-JODENDOM.
NAAR EEN IDEE VAN D-.E.TAUBERT.SAMENSTELLING: FRITZ HIPPLER
MUZIEK: FRANZ R. FRIEDL

A poster in Dutch from 1941 for a German anti-Jewish film. The Nazis wanted as many people as possible to be prejudiced against the Jews.

HIMMLER

Heinrich Himmler (1900–45) took part in Hitler's attempt to seize power in Munich in 1923. Hitler made Himmler commander of his personal bodyguard, called the SS (*Schutzstaffel*). He set up the first concentration camp at Dachau and was soon organizing secret police all over Germany. In 1936 he took over the Gestapo from Göring. He then had control over all the German police services. The SS became the most powerful armed force after the army and grew into a huge organization, which ran the death camps. Towards the end of the war, Himmler was captured by the British and committed suicide.

The 'Final Solution' starts, 1942

The mass shooting of Jews in the USSR, in 1941, had shown the Nazis what they could do to destroy them. They now planned to extend this killing, but they wanted to do it in a larger and a more organized way than by shooting.

The extermination camps

During the 1930s the Nazis had set up brutal prisons, called concentration camps, in which many of their enemies were killed. In 1941 extermination camps were set up in eastern Europe; millions of people were to be murdered in them. The biggest was at Auschwitz; others were at Chelmno, Belzec, Sobibor, Treblinka and Maidanek (see map). While the extermination camps were being set up, Heydrich organized the Wannsee Conference in January 1942 to plan the search for every Jew in Europe. The conference decided that Jews from across Europe were to be transported to these camps and exterminated. Like the Jews murdered by the Einsatzgruppen they were told they were being resettled – taken to a new home. This lie stopped people from realizing they were to be murdered until it was too late.

When Jewish people arrived at the new camps, the weak, sick, old and those with small children were taken to gas chambers and killed. Different camps experimented with different types of poison gas. Those who were fit were worked to death in camp factories, with hardly any food. By the end of 1942, 20,000 people a day were being murdered in Auschwitz. The victims were so frightened and confused they rarely tried to defend themselves. The Nazis also tried to keep their victims from knowing what was going to happen to them. They told their victims they were being taken to the showers.

Resistance

In some of the ghettoes badly-armed Jewish fighters rose up against their Nazi murderers. The most famous revolt was in 1943 in the Warsaw ghetto. The few Jews who survived these revolts escaped to join resistance fighters in the countryside. There were also desperate revolts in some of the camps, such as the one at Auschwitz in October 1944. Almost all those who rebelled were killed.

SOURCE 5

In Kiev [in the USSR] the Jewish population was invited to present themselves for resettlement. We had only counted on 5–6,000 Jews, but more than 30,000 appeared. They were led to believe in the resettlement story until shortly before their execution.

Report of SS Einsatzgruppe C, based in the USSR, in 1941.

SOURCE 6

Thank God, I'm through with it. Don't you know what's happening in the USSR? The entire Jewish people is being exterminated there.

Von dem Bach-Zelewski, commander of an SS Einsatzgruppe, who had a nervous breakdown, explaining to his doctor why he was tormented by nightmares.

SOURCE 7

I hereby charge you with making all necessary preparations for bringing about a total solution of the Jewish question within Europe.

The order given by Göring, Hitler's deputy, to Heydrich on 31 July 1941.

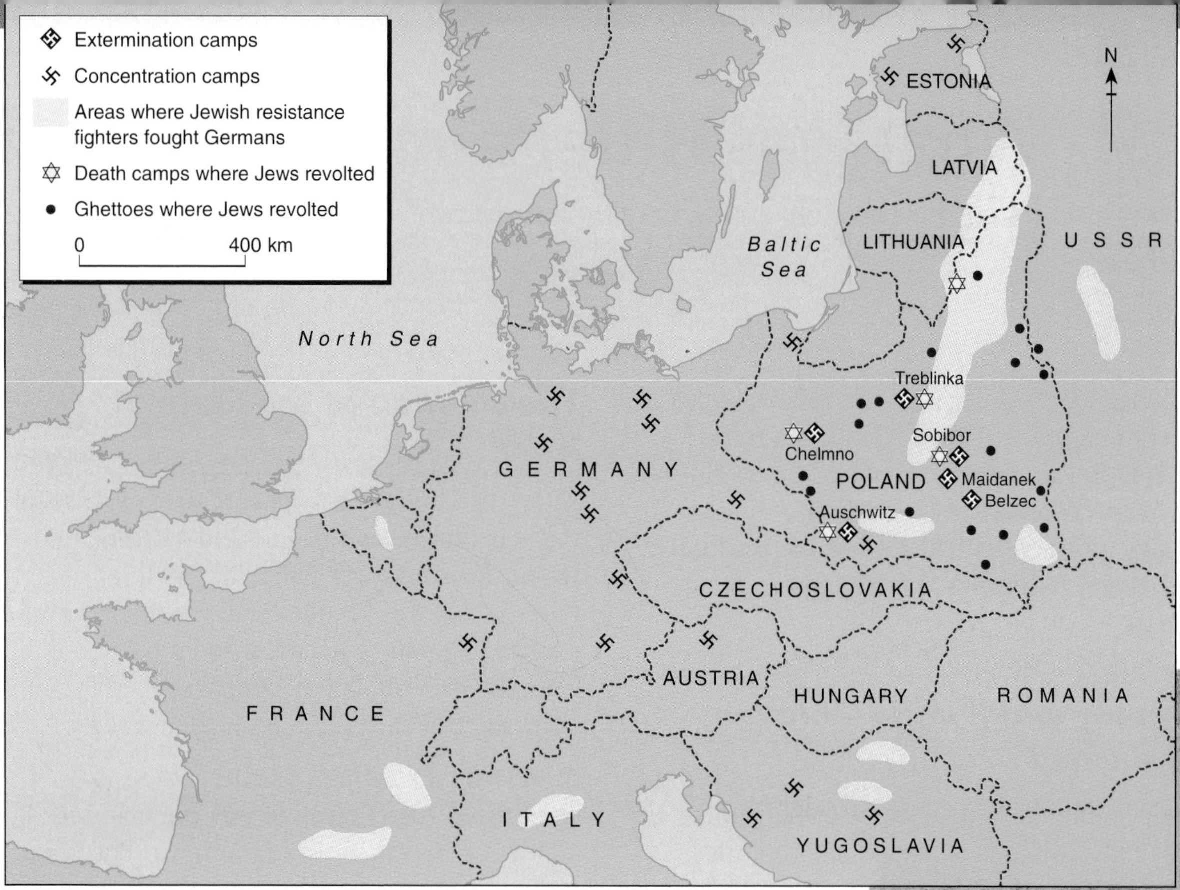

Extermination camps
Concentration camps
Areas where Jewish resistance fighters fought Germans
Death camps where Jews revolted
Ghettoes where Jews revolted
0
400 km
N
ESTONIA
LATVIA
LITHUANIA
U S S R
Baltic Sea
North Sea
Treblinka
Chelmno
Sobibor
G E R M A N Y
POLAND
Maidanek
Belzec
Auschwitz
CZECHOSLOVAKIA
AUSTRIA
HUNGARY
ROMANIA
F R A N C E
I T A L Y
YUGOSLAVIA

Concentration and extermination camps in Europe.

Allies of the murderers

When Jews in eastern Europe escaped from ghettoes and camps they sometimes found that the local people refused to help them. This was particularly true in parts of Poland, the Ukraine and Lithuania. Here some local people even volunteered to help the SS murder Jews. Some Polish resistance fighters refused to help Jews escaping from the Germans, killing them instead.

SOURCE 8

The Führer has ordered the final solution of the Jewish question. I have decided on Auschwitz for this task. You will keep the strictest silence about this order. Every Jew we can lay hands on must be exterminated.

The spoken order given by the commander of the SS, Himmler, to Hoess the commander of Auschwitz extermination camp, in the summer of 1941.

SOURCE 9

I was relieved to think that we were to be spared all these blood-baths, and that the victims too would be spared suffering until their last moment came. Many members of the Einsatzgruppen had committed suicide.

Hoess, commander of Auschwitz, commenting on how 'better' his way of killing Jews was, compared to earlier killings.

HEYDRICH

Reinhard Heydrich (1904–42) joined the SS in 1931. In 1934 he was made deputy head of the Gestapo. From 1941 he was in charge of the area of Czechoslovakia called Bohemia–Moravia. He was made deputy leader of the SS and then put in charge of the SD, the security police of the SS.

Czech resistance fighters assassinated Heydrich in 1942. The Nazis reacted by killing many civilians, including the entire male population of the village of Lidice.

What was Hitler's impact on history?

On 30 April 1945 Hitler shot himself, as Soviet soldiers fought their way through the ruined streets of Berlin, the capital of Germany. The Nazi Party collapsed when he died.

In the years since 1945 historians have asked the question: What was Hitler's impact on history?

Germany and Europe – broken and divided

Hitler's ambitions helped lead Germany into war in 1939. Millions of people had their lives destroyed or damaged by this war. By 1945, Germany was smashed and occupied by the victorious Allies. The total collapse of the German army made it possible for the advancing Soviet army to take over many countries in eastern and central Europe and make them communist. Germany itself was split, with the USSR occupying the eastern part and the USA, Britain and France the western part. Europe remained divided until the early 1990s.

Attempts to unite western Europe

The modern European Union was started by people who were horrified at how the war had torn Europe apart. They were determined that this would never happen again and that the countries of Europe should work together. This has had a great impact on the history of western Europe and has united former enemies.

The creation of the State of Israel

After 1945 there was widespread sympathy for the way that Jewish people had suffered under Hitler. The Jews had long claimed that Palestine, in the Middle East, was their rightful country. Jewish refugees, who had escaped from the extermination camps, started to emigrate to Palestine in their thousands.

At the time Palestine was a mostly Arab country. In 1948 Palestine was **partitioned** and half of it was given to the Jews. The Jews called their new country the state of Israel. The Arabs were angry at losing land they claimed was theirs. This set off a series of Arab-Israeli wars. It has taken until the early 1990s for the Jews and the Arabs to start even talking about settling this quarrel.

SOURCE 1

The USSR emerged from the war more powerful than before. The huge Soviet Army poured into eastern Europe engulfing country after country. By the time the war ended the USSR had engulfed 200,000 square miles of land and 22 million people. Its border was 300 miles to the west of its 1939 position.

*L. Snellgrove, **The Modern World Since 1870**, 1968.*

It was the impact of the Second World War which really stimulated genuine moves towards European unity. The war had impoverished Europe, destroyed Europe's political system and had seen such a collapse of all civilized standards that bold new solutions were thought necessary.

*K. Perry, **Britain and the European Community**, 1984.*

The neo-Nazis

Hitler's ideas have continued to attract people who want to blame other races, or groups of people, for problems facing modern countries. In the 1990s the neo-Nazis (new Nazis) are still at work in Europe. In 1993 they attacked Turkish people living in Germany, who they blamed for taking jobs. These German neo-Nazis have links with similar groups in Russia where, in 1994, Jewish graves were vandalized in St Petersburg. There are similar groups in Britain, France and the USA. Some of Hitler's most terrible and criminal ideas still exist in the modern world.

SOURCE 3

American neo-Nazis at a rally at Washington's Crossing, Pennsylvania in 1993.

Individuals in history

Individuals usually achieve things because other people either agree with them, or allow them to do the things they do. Hitler could not have done what he did without:

- the support of people who agreed with Nazi ideas
- larger numbers of people who agreed with some of what he stood for
- even more people being frightened of opposing him, or who did not realize how dangerous he really was.

During the 1930s he said things that many Germans wanted to hear. His words suited people's feelings of anger and frustration and he used these feelings to make himself ruler of Germany and to impose his ideas on large parts of Europe.

However, the life of Hitler also reminds us that, although individuals need the help of other people, they can still influence people in important ways. The particular ideas and plans of Hitler helped change the course of history.

MONNET

Jean Monnet (1888–1979) was a French diplomat and politician. During the war he worked in Britain and the USA for the Free French government.

Monnet was responsible for many of the ideas which united Europe after 1945. In 1950 he contributed many ideas to the Schuman Plan, which outlines plans for closer links between European countries. This led to the European Coal and Steel Community and eventually to the organization which has become the European Union. This has drawn European countries together in greater co-operation than before.

Glossary

appeasement a policy of giving way to someone in the belief that this would avoid a war.

black market buying and selling goods in a way which breaks the law, often by allowing people to buy for a lot of money goods which should be rationed.

blitzkrieg German word meaning 'lightning war'. Describes the fast type of warfare using modern tanks and planes which the Germans used in the Second World War. The **Blitz** is a word used in Britain to describe German air raids on Britain.

Chancellor the leader of the government with the support of the majority of parties in the German parliament.

communism followers of the idea of communism were also called Marxists and Bolsheviks (after Russian communists). They followed the writings of Karl Marx and later Lenin. They believed that conflict between different classes would lead to revolution. This would be won by the working class who would then control and share out the wealth in society.

concentration camps brutal prisons set up by the Nazis to imprison their opponents. Many thousands were deliberately killed in them. Others were allowed to starve to death or died of disease and over-work.

conscription making people join the armed forces.

democracy the idea that every adult person should have the right to vote and choose the government of a country. Also that there should be different political parties with different ideas and that newspapers should be free to criticise the rulers.

Einsatzgruppen German word meaning 'Special Action Groups'. Sent into eastern Europe and the USSR to murder Jews.

Enabling Act a law passed in 1933, which allowed Hitler to rule without relying on the Reichstag.

'Final Solution' the Nazi plan to murder all Jews in Europe.

Freikorps German word meaning 'Free Group'. Ex-soldiers who fought communists after the First World War.

general strike when all, or most, workers in a country go on strike.

Gestapo Nazi secret police.

ghetto an area of a city where Jews were forced to live.

hyper-inflation when prices go up dramatically and money becomes worthless.

interpretations points of view, different ideas about a question or issue.

Kaiser German word meaning 'emperor'.

lebensraum German word meaning 'living space'. The Nazi idea that Germany needed more land and resources.

Maginot Line a system of trenches and concrete fortifications built by the French along the border with Germany. It was designed to prevent a German attack on France.

middle class people such as doctors, lawyers, and teachers, who are quite well-off but not rich.

nationalism the belief that what matters most is what country a person comes from. Often also suggests that one country is better than another.

Nazi Party began as the German Workers' Party in 1919. Changed its name to the National Socialist German Workers' Party in 1920. This became shortened to the Nazi Party.

paratroops soldiers who are dropped on the enemy by parachute.

partition the division of a country into two parts, each with a separate government.

patriotic being proud of your country.

President person who was the head of state in Germany after 1919.

rearm when a country increases its weapons.

Reichstag the German parliament.

reparations paying compensation to a person or country for damage caused.

Republic country without a king or queen.

SA Stormtroopers who guarded Nazi meetings and attacked opponents. They wanted to replace the army and were led by Ernst Röhm.

self-sufficient when a country has all the resources that it needs.

socialism the idea that the government should intervene to change society and share out the wealth more equally. Less extreme than communists. In Germany the socialist SPD and communist KPD were bitter rivals.

Spartacists name given to groups of German communists who tried to take control of Germany in 1919 and failed.

SS originally the bodyguard of Hitler, after the destruction of the SA they gradually came to control the police, the concentration camps and extermination camps. The Waffen SS fought alongside the regular army. The leader of the SS was Heinrich Himmler.

Index